The Truth Behind Bestsellers

Simple tips, Amazing Results

Introduction

Thank you for deciding to read this book. It is my belief that it will be of much help to you as the reader in your sales career. "The Truth Behind Best Sellers" covers the different aspects that make a salesman successful. Please read on and move your salesmanship to the next level.

What will come to your mind when you think of the word 'salesman'? Well, what I immediately think of is an overly-excited person trying to pressure me into buying something that I really don't want! Have you ever had that experience before? I believe we all have. In fact, that's why we hate getting those telemarketing calls, right? Because we know that their goal is to sell to us something we don't really want.

Are you that person? Are you the person that everybody runs away from when you approach them? Do people quickly hang up the phone when they find out that it's you on the other end? ("But, Mom! I'm just calling to say 'Hi'") Are you finding it challenging to get your friends and family to hotel meetings or home presentations? And, is it difficult to get people (even your own mom) to buy your products or services?

If that's so, take a serious look at yourself in the mirror. Because that salesman that you don't particularly like, is exactly what you have become! Yes, if any part of the above description fits you, then the plain truth is: you are a SALESMAN! And as you can see, being a salesman is not getting you any results!

"But, wait a minute!" you might say. "Isn't Network Marketing all about sales?" "Don't we have to sell things to actually make money in this business?"

The answer to that is 'Yes' and 'No'. But it's simple. Here's what I mean. Yes, one has to sell the services or the products to the prospect so as to make the kind of money one thinks of. But, before you even think about selling anything to anyone, you must have learned how to market, first. Yes, keep this in mind: Sales and Marketing have to ALWAYS be tied together. You shouldn't have one without the other. Here's why:
To have a business of any type and succeed, you must keep in mind this fact: "Nobody likes to be sold. But everyone loves to buy!" Let me repeat, this is the most critical part of a successful, long-term business):

'Nobody likes to be sold. But, everyone loves to buy."

This fact highlights the HUGE importance of knowing how to market. My definition of Marketing is this: "The act of finding out who wants what you have to offer." That's it! Here's how the process SHOULD go:
Instead of approaching your friends and family who have not shown any interest in what you have or are offering, you need to:

1) Find out who is actually looking for what you have to offer. (That's what marketing is. And there are a few different ways of doing this. I'll share with you the ways that I personally have used in my business, that are incredibly effective.)

2) Give them what they're looking for. (This is what sales is.) That's it, guys. It's simple in concept. (But within these two steps, there are quite a few pieces of the puzzle. But they're easy to implement and master. And I'll be sharing these in further training.)

But, the point that I want you to glean from this is that sales are the natural ENDING to the process. Sales are simply the part where you take the order. It's what I consider being as customer service. If you market first, then you'll only be focusing your time on people that want to listen to you - people that want what you have.

Then, after they find out you have what they want, you take the order. You may have to answer a few questions they have. They may have a few fears in getting started. But the point is, they're essentially ready to get started. They're willing to buy.

I'm telling you, my friend: growing a successful long-term business is SO much easier when you're only talking to people that want what you have. And truly, many times they will come after YOU instead of you chasing them around. And you won't have to twist anybody's arm. In fact, after they plop their credit card in front of you, many times they will thank you for allowing them to buy.

So, instead of just approaching anybody, remember: If you market first, then sales will be the natural next step. Keep that in mind, and you will save lots of time, money and embarrassment. And the people that you put in your business, in general, will stick around for the long-run.

This book has some very useful tips for all who have a passion for salesmanship. Therefore, I encourage you to read it with an open mind.

Table of contents

Chapter 1: First things first

Discovering the best ways to be a fantastic salesman is a great skill to discover. Yes, you could be willing to learn the means to offer because of your existing line of work, but learning the trade can be an important device in lots of things you come across in everyday life. People attempt to sell you things daily. If you are in their shoes, you will understand where they are coming from, but after you discover the best ways to sell yourself, you comprehend why they say the things they do, and you understand the exact ways to counter their statements, and address their concerns to ensure you get what you want from the offer!

The most crucial thing in my point of view is when it involves offering is that, as a salesperson you have to emanate confidence. No, you don't want to be cocky or self-important, but you do should have a specific behavior about yourself that the client can levitate towards.

How do you get self-confidence? It comes with knowing the products you are selling. Think about something you think you know a lot about … it could be taking care of vehicles, your preferred sports team, or another hobby of yours. If somebody asked you about one of those things, you could quickly lose the thread on about it, throwing out truths, experiences, and thoughts, with no hiccups at all. The exact same must hold true for the products you are offering. Learn them, and have the ability to discuss them in fantastic detail.

It likewise assists to be selling a great item. It is difficult to be confident about something when you know deep down. It isn't that great, or there is something out there that is better. (Unless you're a used car salesman!).

The next things on my listing of how to be a fantastic salesman are the ability to pay attention. You need to pay attention 80 % of the time while talking 20 % of the time. Listen intently to your customers' requirements or concerns. Let them believe that they are in control of the scenario, all the while you are thinking about the best method to approach the client. Discover exactly what they require, and find an option to that requirement.

Make a connection with the consumer. The customer should feel how to be a wonderful salesman like you can relate and comprehend them. With this in mind, you cannot approach each sale the same way. You would sell in a different way to a "biker kind male" then you would to a 70-year-old lady. You have to find a method to develop a trust to engage in purposeful chat. It is very tough to sale to someone that you have trouble building a connection with. Research your customers tone, language, and physiology.

Staying inspired is important especially for one who desires to learn to be an excellent salesperson. Selling is not easy. Some days you may make several sales, and you might go on streaks when you offer little or absolutely nothing at all. It is a lonely feeling to obtain in your car after an 8 hour day, having not made a single penny. You will begin to ask yourself why you are doing exactly what you are doing. You will begin to doubt your methods and method very quickly. The sooner you recognize that this is part of the region, that YOU chose, the much better. If you're working a proven system or selling a tested item people require, the sales will come. If you begin to question and stress, your consumers will smell it from a mile away. If you begin to attempt too hard, your customers will automatically be shut off.

Chapter 2: Lie Less Sell More

Don't we hear lies daily? Just give it a thought. The worst part of it all is by the fact that we lie the most to ourselves! Why on earth do we do such?

This behavior is definitely insane despite the fact that people lie regularly. Lying to other people is being selfish. However, it is plain stupid to lie to ourselves. How on planet earth do we fool ourselves? Is it even possible? How is it that we are both the ones deceived and the deceiver at the same time?

One of the reasons why people lie is to avoid being hurt. Others lie with an aim of protecting their self-esteem. So to speak, people tend to have pride as a result of their achievements and to some extent even their lies. Lying is now like a cognitive skill. It is a form of intelligence. The reason behind this is it will take aptitude to know how things are. Eventually, one will know the present and will be in a position to create an alternative to it.

Why should people lie in the first place? Could it be as individuals, we are unsatisfied with what our current reality has in store for us? Is it that we would like to create another or rather a new image for ourselves? Are individuals creating an illusion for life which seems better when in the minds? Some of the few reasons why people often lie to themselves and others:

1. Ourselves: We frequently lie in an attempt to avoid painful outcome and consequences, conflict, embarrassment or shame.

2. Our interests are most likely secondly placed on the most common reason people lie. We lie to acquire what we need or want. People lie to attain material things such as money and non-material goods such as attention.

3. Our image: Definitely, we as human beings want others to at all times think well of us. Yet at the same time, we do less respectable at times. Rather than to admit and to suffer a diminution of other peoples' respect. Many times we cover it up. Having failed to virtuously and courageously act, we lie in to appear more virtuous and even courageous than we actually are.

4. Our resources: We lie to avoid expending a lot of energy or time doing some things we do not want to.

5. Others: Typically, we do this as it is unacceptable socially telling what we might be actually thinking because we do not want to hurt and disappoint the feelings of others. People also lie in order to gain acceptance of others. This is because we want to be admired and loved in a selfish way.

Honesty is a critical virtue to any business success in a variety of ways. As a salesman, when you are honest concerning the good things and also the bad things, you will definitely build confidence and trust in the business relationships you get involved in.

The disadvantage of creating a falsifying image is that it ends up with a negative belief being manifested concerning salesmanship. We pretend to be better than the level we believe ourselves to be in. Telling what is not true will further convince us as salesmen that we are by any chance not good enough. This will lead to low self-esteem on the salesman side. Ultimately low performance will follow, and this is not what we want.

When clients have trust in their respective salesperson, these clients are likely to buy from that salesman again and again. This might go on even when the rates and prices are higher. Clients would prefer to hear a salesperson admit to and resolve issues and not to hear a salesperson making excuses or shift the blame to another person.

A saying goes, "What comes around goes around." Salesmen will give out what comes back to them two-fold. When a salesman finds the business is not where he or she wants or expects it to be, someone's salary is not high enough as expected then try to consider your lies.

Honesty pays off to the salesman favor. It's vitally important for a salesman to establish an honesty pattern in life. Lying will only hurt a salesman chance for success. Even if as a salesman you think that telling lies is key and doesn't bother you much, your subconscious mind always knows it is and it will place the shame and guilt in your life. At some point in life, you will always be aware that you are deceiving others if not yourself. When the feelings of shame and guilt arise, your conscience steps should guide you back to the right direction. In this case the direction of honesty.

How many salesmen tend to ignore the truth? How many salesmen ignore the reality in situations? Salesmen tend to rationalize why some things are how they are. This is at the expense of being honest with themselves. The reason behind this is their self-esteem can't take the truth.

What will it cost a salesman to be honest? The first basic step is to recognize when as a salesman you are not honest with yourself. Then consider being willing to look and see beyond the excuses. Look for the real reasons.

Chapter 3: The Scope of the Market

Knowledge is always profitable. It can take as little as a few minutes to as long as several months. The more equipment and updated as you are, the better the chances of your fondest dreams fulfilled in no time! Increasingly aware of the concept of online commerce, which encompasses both the NSE and trade negotiation of BSE.

They should know how to identify good opportunities in the short term and also be able to pr0tect of unanticipated events. Some online trading platforms offer the facilities of opening an account free trade in India. If the trend is positive, you want to go long (buy) and sell very little.

There are several basic concepts means a successful trader in the short term. So, here are some tips to find the right market at the right time. Section of investors is not limited to a certain group of people who are involved full-time in the stock market, but also employees, professionals, freelancers, part-time workers, housewives, teachers, students, and others. Of course, once you register online trading platforms for equities is likely to be guided what to do and how. You cannot become a millionaire by investing only; you can expect a maximum return on your investment if you know how to choose good actions. We focus on what is to identify potential candidates. Investors increasingly join the money making a career.

These platforms also facilitate trading traders with tips, news trading NSE, trading tips BSE, comprehensive news on the stock market, mutual funds and other investment products. When it comes to online trading, which is almost equivalent to trading on the floor, the only difference is the platform and the process you naturally want to buy shares at a low price and sell them at high prices at a time.

With online trading, giving thousands of investors to invest in the comfort and convenience of your space, the trend has grown much more.

Understand the cycles of all or drawings - the trades of market cycles, making it important to take into account the calendar at some point. E-commerce in India is about how to reach you. The general idea is to show whether a stock is driven up or down. If you know the basics of how to select after careful assessment and if you are familiar with the process of buying and selling of stocks, no doubt turns the tide in your favor!

Share trading in India is considered to contribute to such offers investors attracted to the opening of the trading account and start investing in the project. High expectations you have in mind on how to get rich quickly by investing in the stock market in India will surely be satisfied. See the moving average - The average price of moving an average of stock over a given period of time. Unfortunately, it's easier said than done.

Short-term investments can tend to be very profitable yet can also be dangerous. True is talking about when we hear about the stock market is already responding. Not all the images to help you complete what you have in mind.

Chapter 4: Customer relationship

Any kind of interaction between a customer and an organization, when viewed from a customer's perspective, can be attributed to as a customer experience. It is a measure of the expectations of a client during its period of interaction with the organization in any form. It is how the customer views the whole experience of his interaction. It is, therefore, an important measure of the organization to understand clearly the relationship it has with the customers. Thus, after properly analyzing, if these can be addressed properly then it may lead to high customer retention and loyalty of the customers towards the organization.

Companies can improve their customer experiences by implementing proper customer experience strategies. This can be done by several methods like training the leaders of the organization so that they become customer experience experts. Also, the companies need to follow some basic practices to ensure that they provide a good quality customer experience. Firstly, one should have a strategy designed which will be the base for the whole plan of action that the company takes. Without it, the company cannot focus on any area and will be confused on what and how to measure and deliver the experiences. Customer understanding is one of the prime requirements as it helps to identify who exactly the customers are and what are their needs which the company should focus on. Without a proper understanding of this area even with a good amount of effort a company may land up frustrating the customer.

Good design is the next key area that a company lays stress on. With the help of electronic media, bad ideas are mitigated very early and hence one can focus very quickly on what the customer wants and thus help in the effort to make a perfect customer experience strategy. Measurement is said as the most important tool in the whole customer experience strategy as it is this which helps in quantifying a customer's experience quality and helps in making all the necessary changes. Also, a salesman should ensure that their strategic design for customer experience is a one that is sustainable. This is made sure by proper governance, and hence, one can attribute this to a rule book of the organization which is a must. Lastly, one must make sure that whatever strategy is decided is done after keeping in mind the welfare of the customers. This can be achieved only if the employees of the organization have good values and are completely focused on giving their customers a great customer experience.

Being a salesman involves going around everywhere in every form, which was even difficult to implement. For every salesman, there are certain rules and regulations to be followed. Nevertheless, what is important for the salesman is the customer. In the modern world, people tend to forget that creating a good will in front of their customers and proper planning results to a strong foundation. This is because the source of revenue is a customer.

Whether you are dealing with customers directly or not, it is essential to have a clear understanding of their needs and target the market in the right manner. Today, the business market has taken the shape on a vast level. There are many ways to execute various tactics. However, the customer will always be at the forefront of any salesman for sure. A small retail of any particular product requires issuing to the consumer in the appropriate manner to fulfill their demands. To fulfill the needs of the customer and let the consumer meet with the proper resource is the main motive for any kind of service. A business owner should discuss their products.

Chapter 5: Approach in salesmanship

Does this capture you? One's rational mind might dictate him or her to heed caution. A part of it creates a picture. As for telemarketers, success lies not only in analytical approach but also by using the heuristic method in talking with prospects. Just like how the "Don't read this!" warning captivated you.

Traditionally, telemarketers, through cold-calling, feed the qualified sales leads with all sort of stats and facts. The acronym FAB is their most often prostituted means. They connected with the "features", continue with "benefits" and slowly end to "advantages" with a bang.

The sad thing is that it doesn't work that way. Firing your prospects with bullets of information sometimes won't work like a charm. Professional telemarketers must give customers with the data the latter wants and not what the former likes. It's like a person had been given a bagful of Type A blood when what he truly needed was a Type B.

In sales, telemarketers must craft powerful heuristic frames before presenting the data. The general rule is to make prospective customers respond to what a company is offering. And this entails going deep at personal and emotional grounds. The goal is for a customer to identify personally with the solutions and products. Even the best presenter would catch not fish if he resorted in pushing for the analytical level. Knowing what a prospect wanted to hear and how to deliver it effectively is a better technique. Reaching to what customers truly are longing for will be an easier path to a closed sale.

Sometimes, facts and figures tend to be destructive instead of being helpful. For instance, a telemarketer tried to convince a qualified sales lead that a product works well for 68% of the people surveyed. The sales lead might probably ask what really happened to the 32% and may make deeper inquiries.

When making use of the heuristic approach, a phone marketer's strategy is straightly directed towards the desires of the customers.

Let it be a constant reminder to any salesman that customer loyalty is always dependent on the degree or level that someone tends to identify with a solution. The pros and cons of such a solution to both professional and personal success of institutions or individuals. The core issues that a telemarketer must understand are the cause, vision, impact and critical issue. When all these factors are known, the difficulty of connecting with a customer is reduced or eliminated.

According to Dave Brown, a principal consultant with Ridge Global Marketing, when using the heuristic approach, three components are to be realized- probe, pitch and provocation.

Catching the prospect's attention is what the probe does. On the other hand, the pitch talks about the solution you are offering. Lastly, the provocation speaks of the urgency to act (whether there's a budget or not). Selling can begin by building these frameworks and facts and figures can be inserted later on. Let's use a broadband provider as an example:

The Probe: A prospect is paying a fixed monthly Internet utility expense even when such customer uses it only once a week. The unused portion could be utilized to another payment.

The Pitch: The telemarketer relayed to the customer that the broadband provider has a program of charging only the number of hours used. As a result, costs will be reduced.

The Provocation: The telemarketer persuades the prospect to buy the broadband kit with a discount to solve the problem immediately. The line which will get one in touch with clients and prospects is by establishing an emotional response. Getting their attention will help you make them more attentive to your presentation of facts and figures.

How often have you planned your sales strategy around a previous quarter's result or the latest competitive wins rather than building a well-planned strategy built upon the data-driven analysis of historical trends and future predictions?

Best Practice: Understand the Sales Analytics Requirements of Field Sales, Inside

Sales, Partners and Management:

Sales analytics provide advantages to all divisions of a sales organization, be it executives, sales managers, partners or front-end sales representatives. Analytics provide insights on progress to quota-carrying salespeople in creating a plan, the quality of leads and opportunities, liabilities, and the growth potential of accounts or prospects. Similarly, analyzes of information extracted from various systems can be leveraged to enable sales management better prepare and direct sales actions.

From the perspectives of usability and practicality, the ability to modify a quote can allow salespeople to understand what other products can be proposed and what price can be revised to achieve profitable margin range. Visibility can be explained by how well the analytics solution provides access to key insights for the targeted users within the required time to make an informed decision. Sales organizations should take measures while adopting new sales analytics technologies like capturing sales user requirements, piloting with a small group of people, evaluating data quality tools, using an agile approach to capturing feedback and respond to users.

Please leave a review for this book. This is to help me as the author knows to what extend this writing has impacted on you as the reader.

Chapter 6: Motivation

How does a sales manager or a business owner motivate their salespeople? Where should the motivation be obtained from? With so many myths about motivation, as covered in last month's Motivation and Sales Performance Part 2a Sales Myths it can be quite perplexing.

Let's face it motivating salespeople is no easy task. It is a job that never ends and requires you to have a high level of self-motivation and commitment to every salesperson in your team.

Motivation is an inner drive, an energy that propels a person into action to achieve a goal. It can be influenced by internal and/or external factors. These are referred to as intrinsic and extrinsic motivation.

Intrinsic motivation

This comes from within and is the desire to perform a task because it is of interest enjoyable and skill is developed that in itself is rewarding. When a salesperson is intrinsically motivated they find:

- It easy to maintain focus

- They want to do well because the task is enjoyable

- They will do the task even if they don't get remunerated for it

- The commitment to master the skill and be the best they can be

- Enjoyment because they are in control of what they are doing

Intrinsic motivation can only happen if the salesperson is happy to do the task. It doesn't work if they are feeling down.

Extrinsic motivation

Working hard particularly when times get tough along the journey to winning the award is not something a salesperson will delight in. But the thought of winning the award can keep them going.

Designing an extrinsic incentive is easier than motivating intrinsically. With an extrinsic incentive, focus salespeople on the goal and the reward and not on the process of how to get there. Always take into consideration that:

- Salespeople who won't be motivated by the reward. If so what can you do to convince them or modify the reward?

- Possible shortcuts a salesperson may take to win and the ramifications of such action

Sales management's greatest challenge is to implement an extrinsic motivator that has to mean. The extrinsic motivation can be internalised and become intrinsic if it complements the salesperson's values and beliefs. As sales management learn and understand their salespeople better, this will become easier.

Reinforcement

Reinforcement is designed to encourage the salesperson to repeat certain behaviours without reinforcement the likelihood of repeating the desired behaviour is diminished. It's about creating an environment that the salesperson likes and wants to be in or punishment which is to create an environment the salesperson dislikes and wants to avoid. Noticing what a salesperson does is often an indicator of the type of reinforcement used by sales management.

Positive Reinforcement

Positive reinforcement is a reinforcer used after a particular behavior that strengthens the behavior. Positive reinforcement is more effective in terms of altering behavior and therefore the chances of the salesperson's repeating the desired behavior in the future is far greater. There are 3 types of positive reinforcers:

Social reinforcers - Any public recognition such as an award presentation

Activity reinforcers - For example the conversion ratio of customer calls to orders confirmed

Intangible Reinforcers - These are the acknowledgments for a job well done. Salespeople don't tire of being given praise or recognition when it comes from the 'heart.' For example "Sandy, I thought you did an excellent job in handling that difficult customer, particularly the way you empathized with their situation."

Negative Reinforcement

Negative reinforcement is designed to stop or avoid an unwanted condition so as to increase the strength of the desired behavior. For example, a salesperson attends quickly to a customer complaint to avoid their aggressive manner. The strengthened behavior is the salesperson's quick action. Negative reinforcement is not punishment with which it is often confused.

Both positive and negative reinforcers have the same effect: they both strengthen particular behaviors.

Punishment

The traditional view of punishment is about modifying a salesperson's undesirable behavior. Punishment does change behavior but only temporarily and it presents many damaging after-effects in regards to morale and performance issues. Usually, there are clear behavior signs that if they had been addressed earlier mean punishment could have been avoided.

What motivates salespeople?

The most effective means of motivating salespeople is individual. A blanket approach to motivation doesn't work. One of the best-known management theorists is Abraham Maslow, who developed the Hierarchy of Needs.

Abraham Maslow classified human motivation into 5 hierarchical stages. The following explanation of his theory has been adapted into a sales context:

Self-Actualization

These salespeople like to test their personal potential and prefer to work solo to push boundaries. They are solid sales performers and are motivated by being shown the little things that will fine tune their selling skills. They tend to be impatient with sales managers who can't add value to their sales performance

Ego

These salespeople are driven to achieve social status and recognition within the sales force by winning sales awards. Whilst they can be outstanding sales achievers they rarely succeed as a sales coach.

Belonging

These salespeople can be preoccupied with social relationships and therefore become too concerned with being accepted by their customers. They are usually reasonable sales performers

Security

These salespeople are rarely successful because they are too concerned about their job security. Motivation is difficult unless they progress higher up the hierarchy

Basic

These salespeople like to remain in their comfort zone and avoid prospecting for new business. In most situations they are a wrong hire.

Salespeople as any other profession are motivated by different things, so a one does all approach doesn't work. It's up to you to get to know each and every salesperson in your team and understand who they are and what will motivate them to higher levels of sales performance.

Please leave a review for this book. This is to help me as the author knows to what extend this writing has impacted on you as the reader.

Chapter 7: Embrace Competition

Regardless of whether it is intentional, if you are trying to sell a product, you have taken steps to position your product in your market. You have established the price of your product and are trying to attract customers. However, have you really put any thought into the position of your product?

All businesses open their doors with an intention to sell and have at least a minor idea of what their anticipated client is like. However, hardly any spends the time to determine how their individual merchandise or approach to advertising the product will differentiate them from competitors. This differentiation is their place in the marketplace, and generally determines the company's triumph.

A company generally positions itself to fully pull their merchandise and their market. Whether they are the "Low Price Leader," or "Premium Brand." The company's position determines promotion strategy, sales price, and the company's approach to promotion. Subsequently, determining a how your company should be positioned within the marketplace is one of the first steps to setting your company and product apart from the competition.

As you develop your business strategy, fully classify your normal customer. Define they're all of the demographics that make up your potential customer base. Next list your competitors, and list exactly how they are positioned to service your client. Do they attain sales by deep discounts; do they insinuate prestige and quality? What differentiates your competition to your customers in your market?

Now take a look at your own organization and offerings. What features of your product are superior to your competitors'? Can you compete in value? If not, can you offer more luxury or prestige? Do you offer more physical benefits? How about added safety, security, or benefits. How may you position your business where the competition can't compete?

The position of your company and merchandise in the market is vital to your success. Choose your position wisely and gear both your price and marketing around this position. Make a conscious decision to position yourself and under no circumstances allow the market to make this decision for you. By properly positioning the company, you will effectively differentiate yourself and your business from the competitors and eventually, maximize your sales.

Sales have always been competition from the get go. People will do everything to get ahead and sell more of their product than their competition. It is the perfect situation to badmouth your competitors.

But, whatever your situation is, never try to badmouth the opposing team. This will reflect that you are indeed one of them. It will indicate you lack the dignity of standing up for what you have been trained to do.

In a competition-filled job, you will have all the strength not to be left behind the competition. In other words, you will have to have the will not to be let down by badmouthing competition. Here are some tips for you to avoid badmouthing your competition as well as avoid getting badmouths as well.

Badmouthing your competition will only bring you down. You have sunk down their level of competition that in order for you to gain the upper hand you need to play their low dirty game. Never play their game.

Look for options on how you can set yourself apart from them in a positive light. Clients will always get the rumors about you and your entire company. This is why you need to put yourself out there in a positive light so that it will instantly crush all efforts of putting you down.

Work more on your positivity. Now that you are able to set yourself apart from your competition by being positive. Take it to your advantage and further yourself from your competition. Not only will you be able to squash all negative rumors about you, but you will also prove to yourself that you are high above them and you will never be like them.

If that does not count, you can always control the conversation with your clients and lead them out from the negative comments into a more positive one. Control your conversation with your clients and focus more on what you should do to make sales.

Focus on your goals rather than focusing your energy on your competition. The more you to get their attention the more they will enjoy you on their crosshairs.

Chapter 8: Negotiate to win

One of the most vital skills in life generally is a negotiation. Negotiation occurs when two or more people communicate. The intention is to reach a mutual and beneficial understanding on a given matter. To an entrepreneur, negotiation skills are a must as you interact with suppliers, customers, investors, employees, bankers and any other stakeholders, whether internal or external, to your enterprise.

First and foremost, you can only be a leading negotiator when you are prepared. You need to consider to advance issues such as the key things you are negotiating for, your negotiation objectives, assumptions in your negotiation, some information about the negotiating party, their attributes including strengths and weaknesses, and what is important to them. Good preparation greatly improves your chances of winning a negotiation.

It is also strongly advisable to work for a win-win situation while negotiating a deal. When you only focus your negotiation on what adds value to you or your enterprise, without considering the other party, hence making them feel cheated, most likely you will not win the negotiation. When you manifest fairness, considering the situations of both parties, you are likely to win a negotiation. Put yourself in the other party's shoes. As an entrepreneur, you clearly understand that business thrives on win-win scenarios. Lack of win-win negotiation scenarios creates complications at a later stage.

Lay emphasis on areas of the agreement early and defer discussing areas of fundamental disagreements for a later time. Psychologically there comes a sense of progress and fulfillment when you agree on several things, and this also tends to compel both parties to proceed and finalize the few other areas of disagreement. Use some wisdom to diffuse stalemates when they occur. In this way, you can keep the negotiation going on for a while.

Have at your disposal several alternatives that you can wisely put forward, one at a time, to ensure you do not leave the negotiating table without a win. For example, when negotiating a price you can have volume options, delivery alternatives, after-sales services etc that can be tied to the pricing and that makes the other party see more value added. Alternatives provide room for comparison and enables winning strategies in negotiation.

Winning a negotiation, whether business or not, also requires good timing and patience. Urgency sometimes is interpreted as desperation and you need to exercise wisdom if you must win a negotiation. Many times also when you are in a hurry you tend to be compromised and this may make it difficult to achieve your negotiation objectives, hence a no-win situation.

When negotiating with people of different cultural backgrounds, you have to consider applicable cultural norms. While in some cultures you can negotiate over long hours, even over lunch, in others this is not appropriate. While in some cultures starting a negotiation with substantial overstatement hence leaving a large room for negotiation is considered normal, in other cultures it is seen as an attempt to cheat. Since your objective is to win you must be careful about this aspect.

Additionally, you should be clear about what you are negotiating for since this increases your chances of winning. While considering this ensure that you leave room for future negotiations. You may need to consider both the short-term and long-term effect of your agreements, for you to a win-win situation. Sometimes what you consider as a losing situation in the short run may turn out to a winning situation in the long run.

Communicate well while negotiating. Understand and make the best use of body language. Negotiate with the right people. Use the right approach for only the right situations. Understand that many possibilities exist in your negotiation. Being an entrepreneur, one needs to be very smart and know means of getting the things they need through the art of negotiation. You can indeed negotiate your way to success if you learn and deploy the right skills and approaches. Be a winning negotiator.

Just as a buyer can employ certain tactics to strengthen her negotiation position and results, a salesman can do certain things to benefit his position and results. It is learned negotiation skills that give a seller advantage and the consistent application of them will pay off over time. Buyers can always go elsewhere and try to get a better deal if they don't like the one they are engaged in. It's what makes selling anything a tough, tough job.

But, there are things a seller can do to help his position. Here we will discuss a few.

1. Make it clear you have the buyer's best interest at heart.

This means to be sincere and prove it. Using over-baked, cliche ridden lines about how much the you care for the buyer and will suffer a loss just to make her a great deal - does not cut it. Buyers see through this and it has the reverse effect of what most cheesy sellers are hoping for when they use this method. Buyers want to know the seller is there for something more than simply making money. Buyers understand why the seller is selling (to make money), so good sellers reveal to buyers there is more to it than just that. Communicating to the buyer that you love what you do, and giving them specific reasons why will go a long way toward lessening the buyer's concern that she will only be sold the most expensive product at the highest margin.

Make it personal. Tell the buyer you sincerely hope she will be coming back to see you on her next purchase because you hope to establish a strong, ongoing relationship. Few people are so hard nosed they will not react positively to a sincere offer of friendship. As a seller, you can make use of the natural human tendency to want more friendships. And if a buyer sees you as a friend instead of a huckster, she will benefit you with a sale and more to come.

2. Take a "Low Key" approach.

A low-key approach is self-explanatory. It means "not high key". A high key approach is talking a mile a minute, asking insincere questions, laughing inappropriately and too often, showing the buyer twice as much product as she needs to see and telling her twice as much information as she needs to know until she buys something... just to get rid of you. Interestingly, most people who go into sales naturally take this approach with buyers. And it usually does not work.

A low-key approach is vital for a seller seeking to use negotiation skills to ensure a profitable outcome. This seller reminds the buyer he is there to assist her - not push her. He suggests products or services that may meet her needs and if they don't, he will gladly refer her elsewhere. He reminds her he wants her to be happy, but not so that he makes a fat commission or profit, but so that she considers him a consultant, someone to whom she will come back to for counsel, or advice.

3. Apply the lever of time.

A buyer can negotiate like a bulldog. Usually, a seller cannot. Again, this is because a buyer can usually walk if they are unhappy, whereas a seller must find another buyer if there is no sale. However, a seller does have the issue of time to his advantage.

Everyone has a limited amount of time. Nothing could be more obvious. Well, for a buyer, this has a cost, because if a buyer cannot make a deal work, she must go on to the next seller, and try again. And if that seller cannot make a deal or does not have what she needs, she must move on again. And again.

For most buyers, this a nightmare. Unless they are simply having fun with the buying process (and some people actually do), there is a strong likelihood the buyer simply wants to find the right product or service at the right price and get it done. Negotiating can be tiring and take away from other productive uses of one's time.

A clever seller keeps this truth in mind at all times. He will engage with the buyer in every way possible, giving her total focus and attention and immersing her in the process of buying as much as he possibly can, for as long as he can, so that she will not be inclined to end the process and go somewhere else and start the whole thing over. As a seller, you remind the buyer how much she has learned about your product or service, how much you have devoted yourself to working through the deal, and how much more you are willing to do to see a beneficial result for both parties.

Now some sellers push this concept by claiming deadlines, such as a sale ending in 10 hours, or competition, such as another buyer who is waiting to make an offer for the same product, but often these are disingenuous methods of pushing buyers to buy before considering further. These methods may work, but if they are false, and a buyer learns of it, you may lose a customer for life. It is better to be straightforward, and tell the buyer about something imminent if it is true but never use it to push the buyer to a decision.

Just as a buyer can make productive use of negotiating skills, a seller can employ methods to give him a greater likelihood of success. Negotiating is a crucial element of buying and selling almost anything, and those who know the principles are most often the ones who realize the profitable deals.

Chapter 9: Take responsibility

Improving overall personal life is important and you can do this by taking full responsibility for your actions. When you have the power to control your actions, then bad behaviors will slowly disappear and you will move on to a healthier and happier life. You have to bear in mind also that sometimes we make mistakes and when you learn from these mistakes, you are improving your personal life.

People have the habit of blaming others for their own mistakes. A not so good line of thinking but it helps them think they can escape from reality. But reality check, it does not. It keeps bothering them. When you stop blaming others, you are on your way to improving your personal life. Take the blame and full responsibility for your actions and surely everything will be great. When you can do these, you will have the ability to think straight and have the initiative to make things right.

Taking full responsibility for your actions will lead you to a better and successful life. It is a great thing as you can master to control your own mind and body. There are risks as well and taking a certain risk might hurt the people surrounding you. So it is important that you learn to take risks and consider the possible consequences it can create.

More so, taking chances is an important thing in life and participating is essential as well. Don't be afraid to speak your mind and don't even hesitate to ask. Don't be afraid to ask questions when in doubt. A person that has the willingness to improve their lives doesn't sit, but they take actions. They take steps in achieving their goals.

Improving overall personal life requires an open mind and acceptance towards the unknown. So broaden your horizons and learn to take control of your actions and know your limitations as Improving overall personal life is important and you can do this by taking full responsibility for your actions. When you have the power to control your actions, then bad behaviors will slowly disappear and you will move on to a healthier and happier life. You have to bear in mind also that sometimes we make mistakes and when you learn from these mistakes, you are improving your personal life.

People have the habit of blaming others for their own mistakes. A not so good line of thinking but it helps them think they can escape from reality. But reality check, it does not. It keeps bothering them. When you stop blaming others, you are on your way to improving your personal life. Take the blame and full responsibility to your actions and surely everything will be great. When you can do these, you will have the ability to think straight and have the initiative to make things right.

Taking full responsibility for your actions will lead you to a better and successful life. It is a great thing as you can master to control your own mind and body. There are risks as well and taking a certain risk might hurt the people surrounding you. So it is important that you learn to take risks and consider the possible consequences it can create.

More so, taking chances is an important thing in life and participating is essential as well. Don't be afraid to speak your mind and don't even hesitate to ask. Don't be afraid to ask questions when in doubt. A person that has the willingness to improve their lives doesn't sit, but they take actions. They take steps in achieving their goals.

Improving overall personal life requires an open mind and acceptance towards the unknown. So broaden your horizons and learn to take personal control of your own actions and know your limitations as well

Chapter 10: Work Smart not hard

One doesn't have to be a rocket scientist to know you can't be successful without the help of other people. Whether one's success story is built as a result of direct help from people, you asked or built via your customers who bought your service or product, the bottom line for all this is that these people helped you in some way to become successful. What did you know that these other people did not? What is it that made you a success?

The smart network marketer

The smart network marketer understands the value of hard work. One of the first lessons learned is how to work effectively and intelligently. The smart networker realizes they can work hard all by themselves and achieve outstanding results; however, they also recognize multiple people working together can multiply the end result. The lesson learned here is exerted your energy in four places: time, immediate income needs, sponsoring your future leaders, and residual income.

Time

The old cliché says Time is money. For the smart network marketer, nothing could be closer to the truth. The best way to work smart and have money work for you is to learn to manage your time through personal commitment, scheduling and knowing when. Knowing when means knowing when to talk to someone, knowing when to make the presentation, knowing when to make the close, and knowing when to walk away. You only want to exert time when you know your client is ready, willing and able.

Immediate income needs

Why should the smart network marketer worry about immediate income needs? There are several reasons why immediate income is critical to the success of your business. As you grow your business and earn more money, you become less reliant on other forms of work or employment to ensure your stability in lifestyle. Immediate income pays your bills, your groceries, in essence, anything you need to remain stable. The more stable you remain, the more effort you can place into your business.

Sponsoring Leaders

One of the greatest ways you can increase your cash flow and the bottom line is through duplication. You already know you are the best in the business; now teach someone else how to do the same. Many network marketers have failed to reach financial freedom because they lost sight of this one, basic fact: you can't make it alone. With most network marketing organizations you also realize higher financial rewards when those you sponsor are as successful as you. Those you sponsor help you generate immediate additional income.

Residual Income

If you have not chosen an organization that offers residual income, you may want to reconsider. Residual income continues to pay you money long after you have made that first, initial sale or your product or service. The smart network marketer works hard to generate today's sales for tomorrow's income.

In order for you to be successful in your home based business, there will be hard work involved. How you perform your hard work is your decision. If you focus on time, your immediate income, developing your team (sponsoring) and your residual income, you have learned how to work smart and had your money work for you.

Working hard at working smart helps you create opportunities for yourself. That's he the key to success in a tight economic climate. Unfortunately many people, including recent college graduates, continue to make one huge mistake, and that's waiting instead of creating opportunity. This dangerous strategy multiplies when you consider the majority of people around you is doing the same thing. Most people, no matter how educated or experienced, wait instead of developing the habit of someone who creates opportunities. Contrary to what most people hear, in this new economic reality working hard doesn't always get the job - or the job done anymore, that includes finding opportunity.

The other school of thought advocates is working smart. I agree with that philosophy to a degree, but working smart alone is limited in its scope as far as giving you the drive you'll need to succeed. But the answer is not just to work hard or work smart. The answer is to work hard at working smart. That's the key to success.

Working hard at working smart will help give you the best of both worlds, it's what I call a double barrel benefit. When you work hard at working smart, you're maximizing your potential to the fullest. You have all cylinders pumping and you're doing it in the most efficient way possible.

Here're 3 powerful examples. If you take them to heart and apply them, you'll find yourself achieving your goals quicker and with less wear and tear.

I. Work Hard At Developing Intelligent Persistence

Persistence is behind every successful person. You can read story after story of great people who failed over and over again to reach success. People like the Wright Brothers, Thomas Edison, even Bill Gates. These people and many others had the habit of starting at the point where others decide to quit. That's call persistence.

But they had another quality most people overlook in additional to persistence. I call that intelligent persistence when they failed they only saw and enjoyed the experience of getting closer to their goals. How?

By learning from each failure. An example comes from Thomas Edison's failures. He admitted to having recorded over 10,000 failures before successfully mastering the incandescent bulb. When reporters asked him how he was able to persist and keep trying after 10,000 failures.

Edison replied in his calm manner by saying, " now I know 10,000 ways it won't work." This attitude kept him going through all the failures, disappointments and frustrations until he succeeded. And developing intelligent persistence will do the same for you.

Here're 3 tips to help you develop intelligent persistence.

1. Practice persisting in little ways each day.

2. Know when to adjust your goals. No goal should be written in stone.

3. Celebrate small successes or progress toward your goals. This will help to keep you motivated.

II. Work Hard At Doing What Your Competition Doesn't Like To Do

This is a powerful way to outsmart your competition. The most convenient way to get an edge on one's competitor, make your boss notice you, or even gain a raise and do what others hate to do. This is a quick way to separate yourself from the competition. All it requires is alertness and a positive work ethic. This one simple but powerful idea alone has personally won me more promotions, raises and sales than anything else I can think of. Why? Because most people will only do just enough to get by. Few people will spare some time to observe what others around them don't like doing and start doing it. So, whatever job or business you're in, you'll soon discover you have little or no competition when you apply this door opening idea.

III. Work Hard At Being The Best At Something Within Your Specialty

This is a powerful technique that can help you leapfrog over many competitors who try and be all sorts of things to all people. The key is to find an unmet, overlooked or ignored need of your target customers and master it. Make that a part of your brand or what you're known for. To answer this question, you may have to survey your customers.

It doesn't have to cost a lot of extra money. For example, you have the fastest response time, or you have the cleanest bathrooms, or the friendliest employees. All these examples are small but can make a big difference, especially if you're competitors are not doing it. Whatever it is, make sure you focus on being the best at it in your local area, type of business or industry. Again the key to this idea is finding something your target customers want that your competitors are not doing or not doing well.

Chapter 11: Embrace patience as a virtue

'Patience is necessary... One cannot reap immediately what one had sown' Soren Kierkegaard

In today's high tech - instant gratification age we forget the basic truth that Kierkegaard shares. Patience is necessary for all things. Whether we are talking to the teenager that expects to leave school with no firm foundation to walk into a six figure income without putting forth the required work and innovative approaches required or a sales person that expects to close every deal without putting in the effort required to nurture the customer and the deal - in both cases we are really dealing with a certain level of immaturity and entitlement.

We need to remind our team members that it does take time and patience for the seeds we plant to grow to a size that makes reaping a profitable venture. Just like the seed that grows into a plant that is ready to harvest - after nurturing and caring - so to our sales opportunities must be tended and developed to the point where we can complete the sale. If we pull the plant too early, we may end up with a poor yield. We pull the same plant too late and the plant may be passed it's prime and only good for seeding the next crop. So too with our sales deals Pus, the client before they are ready and your deal will not yield as much or provide as much benefit to the client. Wait too long and the circumstances around the deal may have changed so much that it may not resemble our initial vision of success.

Given this truth, one must naturally ask why it is that the feeling of instant gratification and quick deals is perpetuated in our sales culture. Yes, there are definitely those commodities and services that allow for the 'one call' deal, yet the number of these do not align with the approach the majority of companies take. It is my belief that this is actually a failure in our organizations - a schism in the corporate culture that demands month after month performance from even the newest sales representative and does not provide sales management with the luxury of time to plant the seeds that will grow into deals. In such a case it is no wonder that uncertainty and self-analysis/fear of the next months cause an unnaturally high stance of burnout amongst our middle management - one could argue our most critical level of management.

The inevitable question that arises for the leadership team relative to the balance of urgency and nurturing deals. How do we, as senior leaders, balance the need to 'feed the beast' (whether this is our shareholders or our next level of management)?

We all acknowledge the truth that we cannot speed a plant to grow faster organically. Yes, we can apply pesticides and genetic modification to increase the yield of the crops - but when we look at the ecosystem of a sale rarely do we have the opportunity to 'engineer' deal for the greatest yield. Yet the demands of the organization and the street drive harder and harder for the leadership team (and by trickle effect the entire organization) to attempt to deliver increasing amounts of profit without investing in the most critical element - patience.

There are just sometimes you can't do anything to change a situation, but the one thing you can do is the plan. Frankly, that's another subject and what I really want to address is how to develop patience. We sales personnel, are an activity-oriented group. As a trainer in sales, one can multiply that let's say by at least two. Being that way is good at times to learn patience.

Patience is not only the art of knowing how but always when in that moment to do the following:

1.) Stay emotionally detached.

2.) Doing what you might tell someone you care about to do if they were in that situation.

When you "own" how to be patient, lots of great things happen:

1.) People will respect you more being that way. So, you'll get more out of your relationships with clients and they'll last longer.

2.) You won't regret what you did. You'll feel good, even proud of yourself, given situations when your patience "shined".

3.) You'll make more sales. I remember a client who would "test" salespeople by making them wait 45 minutes. Many would just leave, only those who waited had a chance. I waited and landed a customer I worked with for years.

4.) You'll learn more about your client, so you can help them more and they'll reward you with introductions instead of referrals.

5.) You'll feel better about yourself. When you feel better about yourself it's an upward spiral as attitude is the key to success in sales!

Chapter 12: Mistakes to Avoid

Selling to groups is the must have the skill of any sales professional in the new economy. The concept of selling one to many as a way to leverage resources does have incredible value.

The challenge is many sales people mess up the opportunity by making some basic mistakes. This is common amongst both new and experienced sales people. The opportunity that standing up in front of a group of your customers brings needs to be recognized.

Here are three common mistakes that sales people often make when selling to groups, which can significantly affect the end outcome. I call these the three Ps.

1. Planning

2. Professionalism

3. Pitch

1. Not Having a Plan

Obvious though it may be to think that everybody plans their presentations, this is not the case. All too often a sales professional will present in an off the cuff style. In the UK, this is sometimes referred to as 'winging' it. It does not matter how big or small the client is proper preparation can be the difference between a client saying yes or no.

For instance, think about what you actually want to gain or achieve in the presentation, likewise the outcome you have in mind. How much time might you be having? Will you be using a power point slide presentation? Will it be a flip chart? What are the key issues that your market currently have that you product or service will address. Who will attend the presentation and of these people who are the key decision-makers. For these key stakeholders what is important to them and how will you build this into the presentation.

2. Lack of Professionalism

Might seem an 'old fashioned' point and yet many decisions went the wrong way because of a perceived lack of professionalism from the company presenting. Though it may on the surface look good to be one of the boys, this rarely in the long haul gets the business. Well, dress code is usually one. When standing before a group, bear in mind that all eyes are on you. Wear something appropriate that reflects the service that your potential new client thinks that they are buying.

If you are using technology, prepare for failures and test everything at least once before the event. Make your slides neat and visible. This is not an article on creating power points. Our advice is always to thinks through what you want to communicate with, using slides. For maximum impact mix up visuals and text. If you know how much time you will have stick to it. There is nothing worse than saying your presentation will last 30 minutes and an hour later you are still not there.

3. A Poorly Prepared or the Non-Existent Pitch

At the end of it all, we all are sales people. We often promote the products that everybody in a room knows. So prepare and let people know what to expect. This will come down to the outcome you set for yourself at the beginning. If you are asking for the commitment you will need a common and shared agenda. This makes it easy then for all parties to move into a buying 'frame'.

A bit like the famous fairytale of Goldilocks and the three bears pitching is all about, not too much and not too little. Overselling and underselling are two challenges make sure you hit the spot. All your planning and professionalism will help you do that.

The above mentioned type of manager is what is referred to as a "leader." Looking back at history, nobody ever describes George Washington, Abraham Lincoln, Martin Luther King, Jr. or Ronald Reagan as people who "managed." They are labeled as leaders. During your lifetime, if someone ever refers to you as a leader, this is a far more distinguished compliment or perception than calling someone a manager.

Everybody is human, and despite the fact that leaders make mistakes, they speedily fix these conundrums and take full responsibility for their actions. Accountability is the biggest part of becoming a leader. Conversely, managers don't want to admit when they are wrong, they have a major difficulty analyzing and accurately pinpointing the majority of the office issues that currently prove to be setbacks to the organization and its people. In lieu of taking responsibility and proactively fixing the aforementioned problem(s), managers like to ignore that facet of their job.

They pretend as if it doesn't exist anymore and continue maintaining the job aspects that really don't need fixing. Managers take the issues, sweep it under the rug and, even worse. They are swiftly prepared with excuses if and when they are confronted regarding the hindrances that they have been continuously ignoring.

In the corporate world, it is widely agreed that turnovers can lead to a firm's quick and painful demise. Therefore, sales managers, or "sales leaders," as we refer to them, must make sure that they make the best decisions possible while keeping the core goal intact - moving their team and company forward to a set goal. It is at this crucial juncture when leaders push forward and managers make mistakes that, over time create never ending hurdles for business success. Below, you will find a list of "don't" or actions that sales managers want to actively avoid on their professional journey.

Training Excuses: "I Don't Have Time To Train"

As a manager, you must always be making your team better. This means being a professor of sorts, thus helping (guiding, mentoring, etc. - synonyms) the employees better themselves via proven, learned and ongoing training tactics. However, what many do not fully grasp, is that as a manager, to train properly and transition into a leader, you must have a trainer yourself. This person should not be in your office.

Setting Bad Examples

Managers have messy offices, take 45minute lunches, shoot at 5:00 p.m., dress poorly, have little to no passion, allow mediocrity to go unnoticed and, due to these factors, set dreadful examples and fail to grow a team both professionally and personally.

Slow Trigger to Fire, Slower Trigger to Hire

Managers, many times are too afraid to use their gut sense when hiring a new employee. Thus, their hiring times are delayed and they never truly attract the people who would be a good fit.

Passing On Stress.

Often, when managers get stressed, they lose their cool and take it out on their employees in an angry, malicious way. This separates the trust barrier between the employees the manager and will not allow the manager to ever truly lead the people under him or her.

Visualizing Employees As Simply "Revenue Generators"

This concept is quite simplistic. Many managers don't care about the people who are under them. Instead, they look for their employees as if they were numbers. If employees feel uncared for, they are quite apt to leave as soon as a better or, sometimes an even parallel opportunity arises.

Conclusion:

When seeking ways of increasing sales, most of the business owners and sales managers tend to focus mostly on ways of improving their close ratios. While doing this is tactic legitimate, improving the close ratio in a sales team can be quite a challenging task.

In other words, the same result occurs with either choice, but increasing the opportunities is an easier path to take versus increasing the close ratio. The process identified and described in the following paragraphs is guaranteed to work because it is built on and around the simple objective to increase opportunities for sales personnel rather than to improve closing ratios.

The increase in sales is likely to be realized quickly once these few, simple additions and adjustments to the selling process are implemented. The additions and adjustments are elements of a process, not a procedure. Consequently, any of the elements identified may be addressed and implemented without having to wait for another element to complete.

Increases face time with outside sales team to present and potential customers. Think of your business as a professional football team. The sales personnel are the running backs. They carry the ball (products and services) to existing and potential customers. The more time the sales team is in front of a customer, the greater the likelihood that a sales event (touchdown) will occur.

Recently a business owner told me that his sales were dropping and he asked me what he could do to turn things around. He said that their company recently purchased a sales software program that worked well with his mail order division, so he employed the software in the territory sales division. The software program called for each sale rep to make fifty calls each day seeking an appointment before heading out to make calls. That's half a day's time! I simply told the business owner that his running backs were sitting on the bench the entire first half and not scoring touchdowns, so he should find others to make the phone calls so his sales team members could optimize their time in front of customers.

Establish a quota or increase the quota of telecommunication contact with existing or potential customers required each day for the inside sales team. As stated previously, the objective of this process is to increase opportunities for the sales teams. If your business has an inside sales team, then establish a daily quota of outgoing calls to existing customers to sell products or to potential new customers to introduce your company and its products and services. If you already have daily quotas, then increase the number. It is amazing what the impact of just one or two additional calls each day will have on sales.

All sales personnel must develop and submit their sales contact plan each week. Every excellent and great sales rep have a plan for the day, the week and the weeks that follow. Every very good and great sales rep shared that plan with the sales manager. Every excellent and great sales rep know the importance of providing this timely marketing information.

Most all other sales reps don't really have a plan for much beyond a day or two. You know, it's the where should I go and what should I make today approach. That type of planning is not beneficial to increasing sales. Some type of formal routine reporting and planning feedback must be installed to assure increased sales.

As a sales manager for many years, I used with great success a rolling four weeks calendar layout report sent to me each Friday afternoon without fail. Week one showed what companies and customer contacts the sales rep fulfilled during the week about to end. Week two showed where the sales rep planned to be and whom the sales rep planned to meet with during the week starting on Monday. The week was planned in full with no blank days, question marks or any maybe.

Weeks three and four were tentative. Again no blank days were permitted, but since these two weeks were tentative plans, there could be some question marks and a maybe or two.

Besides the important marketing information, these reports provided, the sales reps developed better time management skills. It also conditioned them to think and to plan ahead. Every sales manager will appreciate these habits as they are great contributors to closing sales.

Sales reps should act rather than react, as well as rely more on support team members than trying to do it all yourself. When asked, many, if not most, sales reps will declare that their first priority and responsibility is Customer Service. Their actions support the notion.

As we stated previously, the sales rep is the running back who carries the ball for the company. The largest part of the reason why the sales rep carries the ball is that the sales rep by definition is a closer. The sales rep's job is to score touchdowns, or in other words, to promote and to close sales of products and services to customers.

Customer Service is an important part of the sales satisfaction mix, but Customer Service is everyone's job in the company, not just the sales rep's job. Nonetheless, when a customer calls with a problem or a gripe, most sales reps will stop what they are doing and respond to the customer complaint - even if they are at the site of another customer! My view on that behavior has always been that there is nothing or no one more important to me than the customer I am with at the time.

Additionally, some sales reps will go as far as to deliver customer orders instead of relying on traditional delivery methods. This is a really bad practice, especially if the sales rep is not using a company-owned vehicle to deliver the products. There are simply too many potential injuries and accident risks. Fortunately, many liability insurance carriers are strongly discouraging or excluding this practice from coverage.

If business owners and sales managers want to increase sales, then the closers must continue to do their closing duties and rely on support team members to handle delivery and to assist in solving customer problems.

Reduce "Windshield time". When I traveled with a sales rep, I made note of how much time we spent driving to one place from another. At the end of our time together, I would share the total with the sales rep. It was often a staggering number and certainly an eye-opener. Sometimes and often depending on the metropolitan area, a long travel time from one customer to another was just something that really couldn't be controlled very well. Often that was not the case, so I took the time to pass on to the sales rep the lesson I learned from my manager as a first-time territory sales rep. The message or lesson is a very simple one: plan customer calls for each day to be as close together as possible. If the sales rep has an appointment with a customer in Middletown, then the sales rep should spend the remainder of his day in or near Middletown.

Seek and Find New Business opportunities. New Businesses are commonly defined as either the addition of new products to the already existing customers or the addition of new customers. Sometimes reviving dormant sales of products to an existing customer can be classified as New Business as well.

This element may be the most challenging of the process. Sales reps tend to settle into a comfortable routine and to concentrate almost exclusively on serving the needs of present customers. Nonetheless, increasing the opportunities to close a sale cannot be limited to present customers.

Business owners and sales managers must not just encourage New Business sales, but demand it. Sales reps must document their contacts or meetings with potential new customers. A quota of contacting one or two potential new customers each week may be reasonable. It most certainly will be productive. In fact, the New Business Opportunity source may have the greatest revenue potential of all the elements of the process.

Thank you for reading this book. It is my belief that it has been helpful and very much informative when it comes to sales career and salesmanship.

I believe this book has been informative for you so far. Please leave a review for this book. This is to help me as the author knows to what extend this writing has impacted on you as the reader.

www.ingramcontent.com/pod-product-compliance
Lightning Source LLC
Chambersburg PA
CBHW070412190526
45169CB00003B/1229